Low-water's Edge

Low-water's Edge

Jean A. Kingsley

Finalist for the Charlotte Mew Prize

HEADMISTRESS PRESS

Copyright © 2020 by Jean A. Kingsley
All rights reserved.

ISBN 9781733534536

This book may not be reproduced, in whole or in part, including illustrations, in any form (beyond that permitted by Sections 107 and 108 of the U.S. Copyright Law and except by reviewers for the public press), without written permission from the publishers.

Cover art by Mary Delany. Passiflora Laurifolia (Gynandria Pentandria), formerly in an album (Vol.VII, 54); Bay Leaved. 1777 Collage of coloured papers, with bodycolour and watercolour, on black ink background © Trustees of the British Museum.
Cover & book design by Mary Meriam.

PUBLISHER
Headmistress Press
60 Shipview Lane
Sequim, WA 98382
Telephone: 917-428-8312
Email: headmistresspress@gmail.com
Website: headmistresspress.blogspot.com

For Laura M. Volkmar

Contents

Birdless Country	1
Cold Smoke	2
Music	3
Designing Hats	4
Face	5
Ring Finger	6
Clarity	7
Echoes	8
Failure	9
Lunation	10
Low-water's Edge	11
Together	12
Apology to Wrigley, et al.	13
Artwork	14
What the Dead Remember	15
Presidents' Day Sale	16
A Marked Heart	17
Intrusion	18
Pastoral	19
Thinking Water	20
Notes	21
About the Author	23
Acknowledgments	25

By dying lamplight, crickets weep cold threads.

—Li Ho

Birdless Country

Dim in memory, a pair of shadows
stuffed full of vague longings,
like two bats in a birdless country.
Cucumber-flowers in bloom—
this is the world
of change indeed!

Mist opens day
in glaucous shadows, frost closes it—
there in the garden, the irresolute footprints
of crafty fox.

Didn't I see you there,
your tail newly let down?
A simple question that shakes
my heart.

Cold Smoke

I sleep in a cramped bedroom
with my lover and two dogs,
no room for dreaming
unless I open a window,
drift on out into the deep night
on a wisp of cold smoke
that settles over the dark house.
At dawn, blue hyacinthine light
rises from the cut field—
a misty net I fall into.

Music

Twenty-five miles outside of town,
tangled dust churns and churns
along a highway.
Deep in the fields behind stiff hills
dressage horses canter, trot, canter—
docked swooping tails
form a sensible rhythm.
Somewhere in those fields
a woman pays homage
to slight, careful stepping—
ironed hooves so precise
even cicadas with their bent for music,
listen with a new equilibrium.

Designing Hats

I wish I could design a hat for every mistake
I've made. It occurs to me that I'd be making hats

for a long time, not to mention seeing
my hats on others. Oh look

at that one—it must have cost a fortune.
And that one over there—the brown feathers

dragging on the ground. One is made of bark,
another, mud. I lay down naked

in the mud waiting for my thoughts
to decompose, soon I am lost

in the unconscious expanse of small ideas.
I can tell you one thing, my next hat will

be made of spider webbing, pliant, elastic,
and able to heal itself, like skin.

Imagine without it, you wouldn't know
where you end and the rest of the world begins.

Face

Because I am not the same
clean perspective of myself,
I can't quite remember
the raucous, exuberance of a boy, Tommy.
                But I can recall him stabbing me
in the face with a sharpened, first-grade pencil.
No blood, no screaming, no washing
out of the wound I silently endured:
blunt stamp of a blue-green dot—
fixed among the freckles, moles,
and age spots to come.
                Tommy, I would meet you now
with the scar that was given
grateful for all the love
that never occurred between us.

Ring Finger

Under yellow incandescent light,
drunk from long-necked bottles of amber beer,
eyes wild and exposed to the world,
hand flicking, hip jutting,
ash falling from my cigarette—
I dance like this.

"You look ridiculous," he says,
I throw a drink in his face:
the last thing I remember is the shock
before the pummeling,
              thin tissue in my finger shredding,
finger inseparable from hand,
hand inseparable from body;

I creep in the basement,
sneak into his tool box,
cut off wedding rings from the ruined finger
—notice how soft the metal is.

Clarity

I crank down the deck umbrella
but the wind blows it over

just the same. Who can account
for changing weather patterns

any more than I can account
for the small scars on my wrist:

front stoop, razor, red sidewalk ants.
Not like the Nuba women of Sudan

who stipple the journey of their lives
upon their skin like delicate lace.

Is that a bird in the planter
or just a dead leaf flapping in the wind?

Echoes

You sip on NyQuil, but you're not sick
or are you? It's embarrassing. Maybe

you're in some kind of terrible trouble.
Someone told you once you're impossible

to live with even on a good day, but no one
believed it. Dead drunk, or almost, you slam

into the bridge abutment, jettison
out the driver side window, jagged

spears of glass litter the pavement—
ruptured aorta, severed spinal cord—You lie

on the road counting pebbles one by one
until help arrives while the echo of the crash

circles the landscape before settling
like the rough blanket my mother made,

blue square by blue square, covering
the scene, a patchwork sky.

Failure

The flat-bottomed clouds of summer—
a low pressure system—
obscure birds who remain
mere specks on a distant landscape.
Naked against the river's surge,
lasting regret at failing to swallow up
the day's grief.
Higher up, blue black hues blend
into heaven while roots of dry grasses
writhe and writhe.

Lunation

In lunar August, we spread her ashes
among the trees in the orchard,
I stop to fasten my hair with a clip,

offer slender prayers up and down
the rows: farewell, farewell
dear sister—goodbye.

Who can remember or yet understand
how the stars are pulled down to the vast ocean,
moon that bobs in its ebb and flow,

or a mother wailing into dusky light
having gained only a drifting image:
a feather in a bowl of water.

Low-water's Edge

The moon far off, a ruined rock—
only on earth are vicissitudes suffered.
Each day begins as a new curve on the horizon,
spring is far behind
and brocaded autumn,
strewn with red leaves
and chrysanthemums
so bare and gloomy at low-water's edge,
is fading now.
Capped waves break inland
with a wrath
of who knows what:
the longing of millions?

Together

When drunk they lapse
into indecent vernacularisms—
some specialize in football.
We raise our arms in praise.
I have long been done with it all—
the drink, the indecency, the praise
—this morning I have forgotten
the names of trees, grasses, insects.
I call to the birds:
nature makes no response.

Friend, with your head drooping
in your up-turned hoodie,
how shall we hold ourselves together,
acquiesce in this autonomous
marching on?

Apology to Wrigley, et al.

The clouds whisper
a fine spray of drizzle—not bad

you think—but still rain.
Might be welcome on a hot day,

but late November shrinks
the skin with cold. It's not a matter of *if*

we get breast cancer, but *when*.
After the lumpectomy, she asked to see

the offending tissue—it looked like
an old piece of chewed gum:

gray, slick, bitten.

Artwork

Tattooing technology is based on the design
of the doorbell: quick poking action

injects ink into skin driven by
an electric circuit.

My mother's tattoo, etched
under her right collarbone so

the oncology techs would know exactly
where to put the plexi-glass shield,

was even more primitive. A rectangle
of indistinct dashes she called her artwork:

hardening and blackening with each treatment
into dark birds that cannot fly.

What the Dead Remember

If I had known I'd be dead this long,
I would have brought my Native

American jewelry, tube of lipstick:
Ravish Me Red and some cigarettes.

Daughter, do you remember I wore
a bright green sweater, pants,

and socks—for luck—as I laid out
my turquoise necklace & earrings,

bronze eagle pendant, beaded bracelets,
on the radiation table for the attendant

to see, the oncology room dimly lit?
"That's Zuni and that's Navajo."

"See the difference
in design?"

Presidents' Day Sale

In the black night of a dream
you follow the stars home

except home isn't home anymore
instead a wire dog crate

you enter making yourself small
curling up in the blankets.

The next thing you know
you stop breathing and it's almost over

the only problem
a blinking star that won't stop

so you open your eyes
and there by your bedside

is the ghost of your mother
who tells you to get up, stop

wasting time because tomorrow
won't wait for such nonsense—

the stars, the dogs—your life
is almost over. You get up

pass out flyers: Presidents' Day Sale
20% off everything.

A Marked Heart

Montefalco, Italy,
home of St. Chiara of the Cross,

the withered heart, *Il Cuore*.
We know it was enlarged

from the greedy surgeons who slit
her heart open, eyeing the scene:

bloody crucifix, size of a thumb.
I swallowed my parents' house,

once, after they died,
room by empty room—

If you opened my heart, a portrait:
burnt orange living room,

bottle of pills. Grief imprints us
the same way ecstasy does,

like a lonely woman padding around
an empty house, closing a cupboard,

putting away milk, washing
a dirty spoon.

Intrusion

One last walk through the kitchen
reveals moonlight splashed
all over the floor—
I couldn't mop it up
if I wanted to.

In the morning, I swallow my sanity
in a blue and white capsule
but the darkness scoops me up
like a fisherman netting his trout—
the victim always implicated.

Outside, rain drizzles my glasses
blurring the backyard,
muffles the voices: *tend to me, tend to me.*
Look how the ghetto ivy creeps
under the fence.

Pastoral

Color fades from a dusty window, the sun faint,
a line of trees dangle leaves like limp arms,
flowers lean back in an evening scene.

In the souls of saints, the cynosure of wonder
stunned by the smell of stagnant bog—
breathing its last.

Somewhere brown cows bow to no one
while a mourner idly adjusts her veil.

Thinking Water

I find myself hanging about
an autumn that can be smelt
around us—
all day the sky is heartily blue.

I shut my book, lean against the wall,
after all,
we are mere water molecules
that dribble from between rocks
thinking water does not flow
forever—

at some point in eternity,
it must peter out.

Notes

"Face" – after Michael Ondaatje

"Echoes" – for Mark Preston

"Designing Hats" – after Mary Ruefle

"Music" – for Kellie Reynolds

About the Author

Jean A. Kingsley earned an MFA in Creative Writing from the Rainier Writing Workshop at Pacific Lutheran University, and lives in Rochester, New York. She is the recipient of the 1995 Academy of American Poets Prize, a finalist for "Discovery"/*The Nation* and The Constance Saltonstall Foundation of the Arts Fellowship. Her poems have appeared in numerous national literary journals and she won a poetry book award for *Traceries* from ABZ Press in 2014, selected by C. D. Wright. She is a recent reviewer for the *Antioch Review* and has been nominated for a Pushcart Prize.

Acknowledgments

Grateful acknowledgment to the editors of the following publications in which these poems first appeared:

Amethyst Arsenic: "A Marked Heart"
Damselfly: "Designing Hats"
Apeiron Review: "Apology to Wrigley, et al."
Cactus Heart: "Artwork"
Columbia Poetry Review: "Cold Smoke"
Foliate Oak Literary Magazine: "Presidents' Day Sale"
Poetry Quarterly: "Face"
Skunk Hour: "Echoes," "Failure," and "Music"
Cumberland River Review: "Lunation"
Birch Gang Review: "Clarity"
South 85 Journal: "Intrusion"
Driftwood Press: "What the Dead Remember"
The Ravens Perch: "Birdless Country," "Low-water's Edge," "Together," "Thinking Water," "Pastoral"
Profane: "Ring Finger"

Headmistress Press Books

Tender Age - Luiza Flynn-Goodlett
Low-water's Edge - Jean A. Kingsley
Routine Bloodwork - Colleen McKee
Queer Hagiographies - Audra Puchalski
Why I Never Finished My Dissertation - Laura Foley
The Princess of Pain - Carolyn Gage & Sudie Rakusin
Seed - Janice Gould
Riding with Anne Sexton - Jen Rouse
Spoiled Meat - Nicole Santalucia
Cake - Jen Rouse
The Salt and the Song - Virginia Petrucci
mad girl's crush tweet - summer jade leavitt
Saturn coming out of its Retrograde - Briana Roldan
i am this girl - gina marie bernard
Week/End - Sarah Duncan
My Girl's Green Jacket - Mary Meriam
Nuts in Nutland - Mary Meriam & Hannah Barrett
Lovely - Lesléa Newman
Teeth & Teeth - Robin Reagler
How Distant the City - Freesia McKee
Shopgirls - Marissa Higgins
Riddle - Diane Fortney
When She Woke She Was an Open Field - Hilary Brown
A Crown of Violets - Renée Vivien tr. Samantha Pious
Fireworks in the Graveyard - Joy Ladin
Social Dance - Carolyn Boll
The Force of Gratitude - Janice Gould
Spine - Sarah Caulfield
I Wore the Only Garden I've Ever Grown - Kathryn Leland

Diatribe from the Library - Farrell Greenwald Brenner
Blind Girl Grunt - Constance Merritt
Acid and Tender - Jen Rouse
Beautiful Machinery - Wendy DeGroat
Odd Mercy - Gail Thomas
The Great Scissor Hunt - Jessica K. Hylton
A Bracelet of Honeybees - Lynn Strongin
Whirlwind @ Lesbos - Risa Denenberg
The Body's Alphabet - Ann Tweedy
First name Barbie last name Doll - Maureen Bocka
Heaven to Me - Abe Louise Young
Sticky - Carter Steinmann
Tiger Laughs When You Push - Ruth Lehrer
Night Ringing - Laura Foley
Paper Cranes - Dinah Dietrich
On Loving a Saudi Girl - Carina Yun
The Burn Poems - Lynn Strongin
I Carry My Mother - Lesléa Newman
Distant Music - Joan Annsfire
The Awful Suicidal Swans - Flower Conroy
Joy Street - Laura Foley
Chiaroscuro Kisses - G.L. Morrison
The Lillian Trilogy - Mary Meriam
Lady of the Moon - Amy Lowell, Lillian Faderman, Mary Meriam
Irresistible Sonnets - ed. Mary Meriam
Lavender Review - ed. Mary Meriam

www.ingramcontent.com/pod-product-compliance
Lightning Source LLC
Chambersburg PA
CBHW060226050426
42446CB00013B/3181